ARM KNIT

BEGIN

CW00500283

The Complete Beginner's Step-by-Step Guide, Tips and Techniques on how to Knit without Needles; Knitting Inspiration Awesome Projects

JENNIFER FINN

Table of Contents

CHAPTER ONE

INTRODUCTION

What is Arm Knitting?

Arm knitting is a unique knitting technique that involves knitting using your arms rather than large knitting needles.

At the moment, arm knitting is a huge craze. It has been linked to mindfulness due of its extremely tranquil, repetitive nature.

If you already know how to knit with needles, learning to knit using your arms will be a breeze. It's almost the same procedure, except your arms take the place of the needles, and each stage is much larger! If you're new to knitting, a simple arm-knit item will help you gain confidence in your skills.

Arm knitting is a quick and easy way to make thick clothes. To get started, all you'll need is some very thick yarn in your favorite color and your arms!

This large-scale knitting technique is suitable for both experienced knitters and those who have never held a pair of knitting needles before. Arm knitting is a technique that involves using your forearms instead of knitting needles to make big knit garments. You won't need any additional tools to finish your knitting projects if you learn how to arm knit, and you'll be able to make considerably larger stitches than you could with regular needles. Big, cozy blankets, thick scarves and cowls, and large floor poufs can all be made with arm knitting.

The knitted fabric's loops are oversized. The number of stitches you can fit on your arm is determined by the thickness of the yarn. Prepare to produce items that are narrowed.

Arm knitted clothing (i.e., garments), scarves, cowls, blankets, toys, and home decor items can all be made using Jumbo and super bulky yarn.

This method is quite common, especially among individuals who live in cold climates. Arm knitters can produce knitted goods in a short amount of time with practice.

When working back and forth, unlike knitting, there is no need to turn the work. The stitches are switched from your right arm to your left arm, or vice versa.

For lefties, casting on the stitches on the left arm is more comfortable.

Although giant or extreme knitting looks wonderful, storing such large goods can be difficult, especially if you don't have enough space.

CHAPTER TWO
TRUTHS ABOUT ARM KNITTING AND FAQs

Truths about Arm Knitting

1. The diameter of your wrist dwarfs that of any knitting needle. ***This is applicable to everyone, big and small, male and female***. In our enormous millimeters, we are one.

   A knitting needle's diameter dictates its size. Millimeters are used in the most accurate and global size standard, the metric. You obtain the needle's size by measuring the circumference of a needle in millimeters, then dividing that amount by a pi (3.14) to get the diameter.

Thus, take the measurement of your wrist in millimeters and divide by a pi to obtain the metric needle size of your arm. Mine measures 45.7 mm. A 35 mm knitting needle is the largest.

2. Your wrist gauge is not just "big-boned," but also big enough for Jumbo yarn, ***a novel concept in the age-old skill of knitting***.

The popularity of arm-knitting compelled, the

development of jumbo yarn in knitting standards. The Craft Yarn Council establishes standards for knitting and crochet yarn makers and publishers, and the Standards Committee created a seventh yarn weight category, the Jumbo, in 2016.

3.   Because jumbo yarns are so hefty, they perform best when made with a lightweight, lofty animal fiber. **Nature is always superior**.

What kinds of yarns are suitable for arm-knitting? Here are five possibilities.

- ✓ Knitted Collage Wanderlust
- ✓ Cascade Mondo
- ✓ Bagsmith Big Stitch
- ✓ Loopy Mango
- ✓ Ohhio Merino Wool

These yarns can also be used with large needles, which are both heavy and cumbersome.

Tip:

Supersize Your Stitches: Fast and Cute Ideas for Size 50s

Large stitches and chunky knitting are all the rage this year, as evidenced by the recent appearance of gigantic chunky blankets, caps, and sweaters.

Knitting with these enormous needles does require some skill and can feel a little weird, especially if the majority of your knitting is done on needle sizes 2 – 6. You might wish to attempt huge knitting; with these colossal size US 50 knitting needles and a gauge of 3.5 stitches to 4 inches, you can easily knit an afghan in an afternoon.

While circulars are ideal when knitting at this gauge, straights may be more manageable. When working with large straight needles, brace the ends of the needles on the couch or pillows on either side of you. The needles are long, and their weight can cause wrist pain if you attempt to totally support the weight of the needles. When working with circular needles, place the project's weight on your lap. In other words, this is not a great situation for knitting on-the-go.

4. While jumbo yarns are ideal for arm knitting, they are far from the sole option. You just need to rethink your approach to stash management... and, while you're doing it, perhaps break yourself out of a knitting rut.

    You can arm-knit with many strands of yarn. Go through your stash and pull out some thick yarns, hold them together, and try an arm-knitting technique. This method allows you to create some wild, funky, thick fabrics! If you're constantly drawn to handpainted sock yarn and top-down shawls, shake things up with a graffiti arm-knit cowl!

5. You are not as graceful as you believed. And that is fantastic.

Arm knitting is comparable to hula-dancing at Burning Man. Consider what that might look like, then add gigantic yarn to the woman's limbs. Now imagine her becoming tangled and starting and stopping sporadically, as someone is eating curry while a distant didgeridoo plays, and you may imagine what I look like arm-knitting (and where I live, for that matter). You should absolutely join me in this uncomfortable dance. Emancipate your ego.

6. Giant stitches resemble sculpture; sculpture is a fine art; therefore, arm knitting qualifies you as an artist.

This is very freeing — disregard functionality. Consider expression; experimentation; the possibility of creating a yarn portrait. Allow yourself to become entangled and messy in your own vision, and perhaps you'll wind up with a gallery opening and a studio, and you'll forget you ever met any real knitters.

7.   It doesn't stop there — arm crochet is also an option.

8.   Knitted fabric has a wonderful structure.

It's easy to see how complicated and powerful this inter-looping structure is when examined at arm-knitted scale.

9.   "How do I weave in this end?" is a metaphor for life

on this scale, and the answer is that sometimes you just can't.

If you don't want loose ends, you can use a tapestry needle and finer yarn to sew it to itself. This offers you a sense of closure, which is fantastic.

10. We all accomplished knitters. All knitting is authentic. Rise to your feet!

Who is not a true knitter? That lady on the metro with her head buried in her phone. She could have been knitting at the moment.

FAQs

After you've tried your hand at arm knitting, you're bound to have some questions.

1. **Can I put down an arm knitting project in the middle of it?**

    What do you do when your doorbell rings when you're elbow-deep in a merino wool scarf, or you suddenly feel the desire to reclaim your arms as arms instead of enormous knitting needles? Arm knitters, rejoice, pausing in the middle of a project is not only doable, but also shockingly simple.

Simply place each stitch on a stitch holder one by one. It is suggested that stitches be put onto a cardboard gift wrap roll. If you don't have one, you can also use a long leftover piece of yarn to make the stitches. Keep track of which arm your last row of stitches was on, so you can immediately resume work when you're ready.

2. **How can I make my stitches tighter?**

Arm knitting produces looser, chunkier stitches than traditional knitting, but try to keep your stitches as close to your hand as possible to achieve more consistent stitches. Make sure each stitch is snug around your arm, but not too tight to become uncomfortable. Pull each stitch slightly tighter as you knit, and try to keep your hands together as much as possible. You'll start to develop muscle memory and, like in old-school knitting, you'll soon be able to make more consistent stitches without even trying.

3. **How does one knit with strands of yarn?**

Knitters frequently double, triple, or even quadruple thinner yarn to generate chunkier yarn. When casting on, start with multiple balls of yarn and hold the ends of each strand together. Continue knitting from separate balls of yarn, as winding the strands together beforehand will almost certainly result in a knotted mess.

CHAPTER THREE

ESSENTIAL TIPS

Tips before Getting started

1. Choose whether you want to work with synthetic or natural fibers. What is the desired bulkiness of your garment/blanket? This determines the yarn's weight. Chunky, Bulky, Super Bulky, and Jumbo are the best yarn weights. Roving is a term used to describe super bulky or jumbo yarn.

2. What kind of look do you want to achieve? Do you want to work with a single

bulky yarn or a mix of several yarns strung together in 3 to 4 strands?

3. If you're following a pattern, the ideal yarn weight/types to use are usually suggested.

4. The number of stitches you can fit on your arm is determined by the thickness of the yarn. Prepare to produce items that are narrow. If you're redecorating your bedroom and expecting something to fit the entire length and width of a queen-size bed, you might be disappointed.

5. Your stitches will not be perfectly even. Your arm's diameter ranges from the wrist to the upper arm. That's fine! Arm knitting's general loose weave is more rustic, which adds to its charm. The loops resemble those on size 50 needles in appearance.

Tips when Ready to Start Arm Knitting Session

1. Make sure the yarn you're using is entirely unwound from the skein before you begin. While making the stitches, you must twist the

yarn. Knots will occur if the skein is not unwound.

2. When working with Super Bulky or Jumbo yarns, such as Knit Collage Wanderlust yarn, use a clean sheet or mat underneath to keep things clean. You'll want to keep the pricey merino wool in good shape.

3. Prepare to give this assignment your undivided attention. It's better not to watch your favorite show while arm knitting if you're used to doing so when you're crafting. Turn off the television.

4. When you need to take a break from arm knitting, have Saran wrap/Plastic wrap on hand. This should be threaded through the stitches, and then the two ends of the plastic wrap should be tied together to secure the stitches.

5. Short-sleeved clothes is recommended. Stitches are easier to place on bare arms.

6. You'll need to leave extra yarn to bind off (approximately a row and a ½). As you get closer to the conclusion of your project, keep an eye on how much

yarn you have left. Because Jumbo Yarns have less yardage, the end of the project is completed swiftly.

Tips when Arm Knitting

1.   Cast your stitches onto your forearms as tightly as possible. That's when your blanket will have a great even pattern.

2.   Cinch up each stitch as you knit it so that it fits snugly on your forearm.

3.   Make sure not to tie your hoops too tight when you cast off (at the conclusion of the knitting process), but rather loosely.

CHAPTER FOUR

HOW TO ARM KNIT:
INSTRUCTION 1

Casting On

1. Begin by knitting with three strands of yarn at the same time, treating them all as one thick yarn strand. Leave a yarn tail of about 1 m (1 yard) for every 10 stitches for cast-on stitches. Make a slip knot and tighten it around your right wrist. The working yarn goes from your arm to the yarn balls. The chopped (short) end is referred to as the tail.

2.   Make a loop with the tail so that the rest of it hangs in front of it.

3.   With your right hand, grasp the top of the loop. Grab the

working yarn with your left hand through the loop.

4.　Pull through the loop, the working yarn. Drop the yarn (tail) that you've been holding in your right hand.

5.   Put over your right hand, the
      new loop you've made.

6.   To tighten the stitch on your
      arm, pull the working yarn
      and tail apart. To add cast-
      on stitches, repeat Steps 2 –
      6.

Knitting from Right Arm to Left Arm

1. Take the working yarn in your right hand and place it over your thumb. Over the working yarn, close your fist.

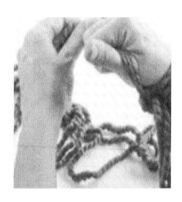

2. Pull the first stitch from your right arm over your fist while holding the working yarn in your fist.

3. Drop the previous stitch once it is over your fist. The working yarn has formed a new stitch by passing through the previous one.

4. Place the new stitch on your left arm after turning it a half turn clockwise in your right fist. Giving your stitches a half turn as you proceed will prevent your fresh (, or new) stitches from twisting.

5. The nearest section of the loop or stitch (the leg) to you should extend to the working thread. For the remaining armful of stitches, repeat

steps 7 – 11. To maintain the stitches taut, grasp the working yarn near to the hand/arm to which you are shifting your stitches. Tighten the stitch just before the last one by pulling on the working yarn until it is snug against your arm, following the completion of a stitch. Keep your stitches as bunched up and as close to your wrist as possible when working with many of them. As you go closer to your elbow, your 'needle' becomes more inconsistent.

Knitting from Left Arm to Right Arm

1. It is similar to right to left knitting; the only difference is that you are knitting in the opposite direction. Close your fist after placing the working yarn over your left hand's thumb.

2. Pull the first stitch from your left arm up and over your left fist with your right hand.

3. Drop the, old stitch and turn the loop in your left hand

slightly counter-clockwise so the leg of the stitch closest to you goes to the working yarn.

4. Place loop on your right hand, and then steps 12 – 15 should be repeated for the entire row of stitches.

Casting Off

1. On your right arm, knit two stitches.

2. Pick up the first stitch you knitted on your right arm, and pull it over the last stitch you knitted, with your left hand.

3. Repeat Step 17 after knitting the next stitch from your left arm. Steps 17 and 18 should be repeated until only one stitch remains. Cut the tail to the desired length and pull the end through the remaining loop.

Arm Knitting Styles

Stockinette Stitch Style

Starting Stitching Method: Long Tail Cast

To begin using the long tail cast method, grab your yarn and twist the tail yarn before reaching through the loop you just produced and pulling the yarn to tie it. Repeat these steps as needed for as many stitches as you require.

Grab the live yarn and draw it through the first stitch (loop) and lay it flat with the row of stitches you have from the long tail cast starting method. Repeat this step with your remaining stitches (loops) until your row is finished. You've got yourself a stockinette stitch!

Closing Stitching Method:Loop on Loop

Take the last loop on the end and stretch your hand through, grasping the next loop and slipping the last loop over it to tie off your stitches (loops). Repeat until there are no more loops left,

then knot (, or tie) off with the
remaining yarn.

Ribbing Stitch Style

Starting Stitching Method: Chain of Stitches

Take your yarn and twist the tail
yarn, reaching through the loop
you just made and pulling the
yarn, tying it for the starting
method, chain of stitches. Then,
using the live yarn in your hands,

draw it through the first loop. Repeat the process for as many stitches as you need.

Grab your live yarn and draw it through the first stitch, laying it flat, as you did with your stitches from the chain of stitches starting method. Continue in this manner until you've finished the first row.

To make a reverse stitch, draw the yarn through the stitch from back to front, then from front to back. Complete the row and then repeat this procedure for the subsequent row. You've got yourself a ribbing stitch!

Closing Stitching Method: Loops and Yarn

Pass your hand through the last two loops, grab the live yarn, and pull it through the loops. To close off the row, repeat this step. Finish by tying off with the leftover yarn.

CHAPTER FIVE

HOW TO ARM KNIT: INSTRUCTION 2

1. For this project, you'll need two balls of yarn. Measure the length of each ball of yarn four times from your hand to your elbow.

2. Make a loop with the two yarn pieces.

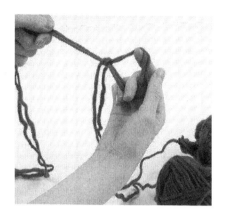

3. Insert your arm through the loop.

4. Pull the loop tighter around your wrist.

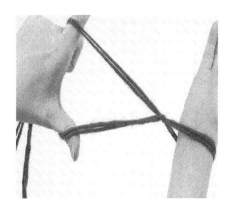

5. Next, proceed to cast the stitches onto your arm.

6. **NB:** While this may appear to be a difficult task, the

technique is the same as
hands and arms as it is with
knitting needles.

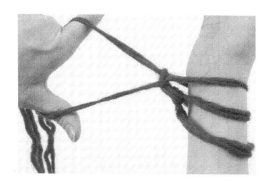

7.   Cast around 10 – 12 stitches
     onto your arm, depending on
     the desired gaiter width.

8. Knitting is done by holding the doubled piece of yarn in one hand and moving the stitch over it with the other hand.

9. Transfer the work to the opposing arm after knitting each stitch, one at a time.

10. Knit in the same manner as before until you reach the desired length.

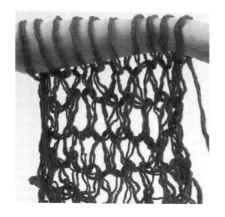

11. Cast off the knitting by knitting two stitches at a time and lifting the first stitch over the second (i.e., next) stitch. Continue along the length of the arm until all of the stitches are cast off.

12. Fold the knitted piece in half and sew/tie the sides together to make a tube.

CHAPTER SIX

HOW TO ARM KNIT:
INSTRUCTION 3

All you need is a positive mind-set and a lot of thick yarn to get started. I use three strands of thick yarn at the same time to make the knit cloth particularly full.

Casting On

Slip Knot

Note*: The yarn that runs from where you're working to the cut end of the yarn is called the **tail**, while the yarn that goes from where you are working to the* *balls of yarn are known as the **working yarn**.*

1.   You'll be working with three skeins of thick (, or bulky) yarn at once. Combine all of the ends and treat them as though they were one strand of thick yarn. Make sure your yarn can freely unfold from your skeins before you begin.

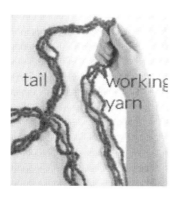

2. Make a loop by taking the working yarn over the tail about 1.5 yards from the end of the yarn.

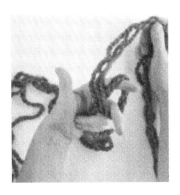

3. Pull through the loop, the working yarn.

4.   Tighten this to complete the slip knot.

5.   Hold the slip knot in your right hand, the tail closer to you and the working yarn further away.

Casting On

1. Make a loop with the tail,
    allowing the rest of the tail to
    hang in front of the loop.

2. With your right hand, grasp
    the top of the loop. Grab the
    working yarn with your left
    hand through the loop.

3.	Next, pull it through the loop, and then drop the yarn that you were holding in your right hand.

4.	Put over your right hand, the new loop.

5.	To tighten the stitch on your arm, pull the working yarn and tail apart.

6.	Repeat this process for as many stitches as you want.

Cast on 10 stitches if you want to make a cowl.

We're off to a great start! You've just finished the most difficult portion. From this point forward, everything is simple.

Knitting

Arm knitting entails knitting all of the stitches from your right arm to your left, then back to your right. You make a new row every time you move the stitches from one arm to the other, knitting as you go.

Let's get started:

Row 1, First Stitch:

1. Take the working yarn and place it over your thumb on your right hand (remember, the working yarn goes to your skeins of yarn). (The tail, or cut end, will no longer be used).

2. Close over the working yarn, your fist.

3. Pull the first stitch from your right arm over your fist while holding the working yarn in your fist.

4. Effectively, you are pulling the working yarn through the existing stitch to create a

new one to place on your left arm.

5.   Drop the old stitch after it is over your fist. Taking the new stitch in your right fist, place the new stitch on your left hand/arm after turning the loop a ½ turn.

6.   The part that goes to the working yarn, should be the part of the loop in front of your hand (known as the front leg of the stitch).

Row 1, Second Stitch:

This stitch is identical to the previous one, but sometimes it helps to see it twice.

A.

B.

C.

Make the working yarn be the front leg of the stitch by twisting loop ½ turn (D & E).

D.

E.

F.

G.   The working yarn is the front of the stitch.

Note: To maintain the appearance of fullness in the cloth, make the stitches as tight as possible while still allowing for movement. Begin the next stitch by holding the working yarn near to your left hand.

H.

7. Continue stitching until you reach the end of the row, as seen in the third photo above.

Row 2, from the left to the right arm:

Working on Row 2 is the same as Row 1, only you're knitting in the opposite direction, from your left arm to your right.

1.   Close your fist after place working yarn over thumb on left hand.

2.   Pull the first stitch from the left arm up and over the left fist with your right hand.

3. While still holding the loop in your left hand, drop the stitch with in your right hand.

4. Turn the stitch so that the working yarn is facing you.

5. Next, put the loop on your
    right hand.

6. Now you're ready to go on to
    the next stitch.

The second stitch is the same as the first, running from left to right:

7. Continue stitching until you reach the end of the row.

8. Knit from right to left arm, then left to right arm, until desired length is attained.

9. Finish with all of the stitches on your left arm. Make sure you have enough yarn to bind off and complete any necessary seaming (at least 4 yards for the cowl).

Woo!! Congratulations! You've covered the majority of it, literally!

Binding Off

1.   Begin with all of the stitches on your left arm (Although this direction is more typical, you can bind off either way).

2.   Knit on to your right arm, two stitches.

3.   Pick up the first stitch you knit on your right arm with your left hand.

4. Pull the first stitch over the last knitted stitch.

5. From your left arm, knit the next stitch. Your right arm should have two stitches again.

6.   With your right hand, pick up
     the first stitch once more.

7.   Bring it up and over the
     stitch you just finished.

8.　Over the top of the fabric, the stitches you bind off will chain with one another.

Tip: *Cast off loosely! Keep the stitches loose enough to match the width of the stitch below when binding off. It's simple to over tighten it.*

Ending It

1.　Take off the last loop from your arm. To prevent the stitches from pulling out, loosen the loop a little. Place your piece on the table (, or, lay your piece down).

2. Cut enough yarn for your project's seams from the working yarn (approximately 1.5 yards is needed to seam the cowl).

3.   Bring through the remaining loop, the end of the yarn you just cut.

4. Pull the loop tighter. It's all
    set to be finished!

Finishing

Use the mattress stitch to finish
the cowl or to join any two ends of
arm knitting together. A mattress
stitch places the seam on the
backside or wrong side of the knit
fabric, giving the front side the
appearance of being miraculously
joined.

Mattress Stitch

1.   Begin by abutting, right sides or knit sides facing up, the two ends of arm knitting against each other. Takes note that the working yarn should come from the top. The breadth of the ends should be the same. To match up evenly, you may need to drag the cast on edge wider. To allow for this, the stitches should, give a little. However, exercise caution in avoiding pulling too far.

2. On the right side, bring your working yarn below the first line of stitches (see the "v"). Bring it all the way through.

3. Bring the yarn under the first line of stitches after bringing the yarn over to the left side. Bring it all the way through.

4. Repeat the process on the right side.

5.   On the left side, repeat the process. Continue until the entire length of your work is seamed. Allow enough space between the stitches that the yarn you've run through seems to be a line of stitches.

Note: *When performing the mattress stitch, the critical step is to locate*

and go below the "v" of each line of threads. Maintain consistency regardless of how you do it or which line you pick.

Weaving in the Ends

1. Weave in the end of the working yarn on the wrong side of the piece after flipping the work to the purl side.

2. On the seam's tighter side, i.e., the cast on edge, weave the yarn under and over the loops.

3.   Cut the yarn after tucking it
      beneath multiple stitches in
      the seam.

Excellent work! You're now free to arm knit as much as you want. I hope it was straightforward and that you enjoyed the procedure.

CHAPTER SEVEN

ARM KNIT PROJECTS

Arm Knit Scarf

1. Make a slipknot to begin knitting a scarf on your arm. Cast loops on your forearm to continue. Cast on 10 stitches (or more if desired) on your forearm using thick yarn. You're all set to start knitting your first row.

2. With your right hand, hold the yarn to be worked. All of the cast-on stitches are also on this same hand.

3. Grab and slide the first loop closest to your hand over the

strand you're holding. This result in a loop.

4.   Transfer to your left hand, and tighten the loop around your left forearm. This is the first knitted stitch you've done.

5.   Repeat this procedure until all of the stitches have been transferred onto your left forearm.

6.   Move on with the second row.

7.   Hold the yarn in your left hand (the same side holding all the stitches) this time.

8. Slide the loop closest to your left hand over the yarn with your right hand. This result in a loop.

9. Next, place on your right forearm that loop.

10. Carry on in this manner until all stitches on the left have been arm knitted on to the right.

11. Knit as many rows as you want until you reach your chosen length.

Follow these instructions to cast off.

It makes no difference the side your stitches are on. Let's imagine they're on your left arm, for example.

12. Knit the first stitch onto your right arm, then the second stitch.

13. With these two stitches, bring over the second knitted stitch, the first knitted stitch to leave one stitch on your right arm.

14. This is very similar to casting off or binding off when using needles to knit.

15. Knit over to your right arm, another stitch.

16. Bring the stitch from your right arm over the newly

knitted stitch once again. On your right arm, you have one stitch. Continue in this manner until all of the stitches have been bound off.

17. Pull the yarn tightly through the last loop. The stitches will not unravel as a result of this.

18. Finish by weaving in the ends. This is something you can do with your fingertips. Cut to remove the excess.

19. You've completed your arm knitted scarf. Takes pleasure in your new-look!

Arm Knit Blanket

1. For your tail, unravel roughly a 5 – 6 foot piece of yarn. On your right forearm, tie a slip knot.

2. Create a V-shape with your left hand using the working yarn, which is the skein of yarn, and the tail.

3. Place your right hand under the left hand's working yarn. Through the loop, pull the yarn from the tail. Take and pull over your right arm, the loop.

4. Continue casting stitches on the right forearm. Make it snug, but not too snug.

Carry on in this manner until 25 stitches are cast on your right forearm.

5. Once you've completed the 25 stitches, repeat the procedure on your right forearm. Pull the first stitch over the working yarn with your right hand while holding the working yarn. With the working yarn, create a loop and over your left hand.

6. Until all are on your left forearm, continue taking stitches.

7. Continue knitting from, left to right, then right to left,

until you reach around 34 – 38 rows or your desired length.

8. It takes more than one skein of wool to make a decent-sized arm knit blanket. Tie the ends together with the least amount of yarn possible to continue knitting.

9. Tighten the knot. Once your arm knit blanket is finished, you can trim the excess yarn. Continue knitting once the ends have been knotted.

After reaching the desired length, the final step is to cast off.

10. As you did previously, knit two stitches from your left arm to your right arm. Then, over the second stitch, slip the first stitch. This is quite similar to needle casting off.

11. On your right arm, knit another stitch. Then, over the last stitch, slip the previous one. Continue until there is only one loop remaining.

12. Tie a knot by cutting off and pulling over the working yarn.

13. Weave the tails into your blanket to conceal them.

14.   Where you've made knots to join the yarn, trim away any excess yarn.

16.   And there you go!! You've got your arm-knit blanket.

Giant Yarn Throw Pillow

Tools Required

- ✓ 2 pounds giant yarn
- ✓ 15–inch piece of sturdy yarn, in a color similar to that of your project
- ✓ 16–inch pillow insert

Instructions

Tip: Three fingers should fit inside the stitch for small stitches. For proper sizing, you'll need four fingers for standard stitching.

1. Join in the Round after Casting On

Make a slip knot after measuring 7½–inch into your giant yarn. To accomplish this, twist the yarn to form a small loop, reach through the loop to grab the yarn, pull it through, and cinch down to form a secure three-finger wide loop. This slip knot is the first stitch of your cast-on.

Using the long tail method, add 12 additional tiny stitches (i.e., creating a series of slip knots). Begin by creating a small loop with the measured 7½–inch tail, then pulling the live yarn (the yarn attached to your skein) up through and snugging down to create another three-finger loop. Continue until a total of 13 cast-on stitches are obtained.

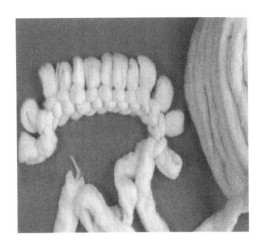

Ascertain that the row of cast-on stitches is not twisted. Then, temporarily pull a portion of the yarn tail through the final stitch you cast on to prevent it from falling out during your first round of knitting. (Once you reach that stitch on your first round of knitting, pull the tail out and continue knitting normally).

Snug the live yarn around your three fingers after drawing it through the very first cast-on stitch. You've now formed the first stitch of your first round of knitting – see how joining in the round causes your item to form a small circle?

2. Begin Knitting Your Rounds

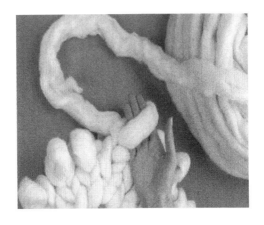

Continue knitting two rounds of small stitches by dragging the live yarn through the loops and snugging it around your fingers (three fingers wide). Then, knit six rounds of stitches of usual (, or regular) size (four fingers wide).

Weave the tail of the yarn through every other loop from the cast-on stitches after turning your work over. Close the opening by gently pulling tight, then insert the tail into the project's interior.

Reverse the work so that you are looking at the interior of the project. The yarn tail should be passed through one of the cast-on stitches and secured with a knot.

3. Add Your Insert

Place, on the inside of your work, the pillow insert. Around the pillow insert, knit two or three rounds of small stitches.

Tip: *Due to the fact that you are knitting with your hands rather than a fixed size knitting needle, the pattern is varied. Determine whether you can easily close your job with just two rounds or if a third is required.*

4.   Complete It

Cut your yarn (leaving enough length), then thread it through your stitches and carefully pull your work closed. Secure the end of the yarn by passing it through one of the last stitch loops and tying a knot. The remainder of the yarn should be tucked inside your project.

Loop the 15–inch piece of sturdy yarn through the final stitches. Close them tightly by pulling, and secure them with a double knot. Ends should be tucked into the project.

Tip: This yarn will be more durable than your giant yarn and will be able to withstand this pressure better.

Now, place that lovely pillow on the couch and prepare for some real snuggling time!

Printed in Great Britain
by Amazon

84394222R00063